Glass Enclosure

GLASS ENCLOSURE

Charles O. Hartman

Wesleyan University Press

Published by University Press of New England / Hanover and London

Wesleyan University Press
Published by University Press of New England, Hanover, NH 03755
© 1995 by Charles O. Hartman
Printed in the United States of America   5   4   3   2   1
CIP data appear at the end of the book

The publisher gratefully acknowledges the support of Lannan Foundation
in the publication of this book.

"Glass Enclosure" was first published in *Temblor.*
"Incentive" was first published in *Ploughshares.*
"The Burden of the Desert of the Sea" was first published in *The Agni Review.*
"Colloquy" was first published in *Quarterly West.*
Part of "Anthem" was first published in *Ironwood,* and the whole poem first
    appeared in *TriQuarterly.*
"The Done Without" was first published in *Pequod.*
"After Kuo Hsi" was first published in *Yale Review.*
"Minnesota" was first published in *Carolina Quarterly.*
"Tuxedo" was first published in *TriQuarterly.*
"The Nation Semaphores Its Intentions" was first published in *Perspective.*
"Gravitation" was first published in *Carolina Quarterly,* and also appeared in a
    limited edition by Sea Pen Press.
"Limpet" was first published in *Southwest Review.*
"Monologues of Soul & Body" was first published in *Tyuonyi.*

Contents

Glass Enclosure

Glass Enclosure

Sky-
light
water
beaded a snow moustache
going under the haze sun say
morning! Know it anywhere. These hands
almost still
the fingers so wise about moving
like a son of a bitch
and fold up sweet.
Step outside
or look twice.
Say in the Bible
Thy hands have made me.
What, hey
what can go wrong?
Elvin got it
Ray got it, days
I got it double. Morning
come to terms, flex, reflex,
yellow light in block chords.
No snow abides
but an alligator kind of thing
down corner and down right side
a drop cut loose. The heat is on.

Where these palms have been
no wonder the fingers fly.
Baby I mean you. Only hard thing
remembering to
breathe sometime.
Fool with it!
Hang the note out there on the fool end and wind.
Sky full of big bluster
with half a brain. Full of fantasy.
Chimneys and roofs of Paris

```
work of my hands flesh
work of my hands grace

work in my hands music
mark on my hands grace

musk on my hands flesh
mask of my flesh music
```

The print's pushed just a little, so the white
of this chair rail has milk's abundant brown
to it: white through and through, as the trees' light
clouded by muslin in the next, last room
washes to dry saffron through the screen door
ahead, down the numinous hall whose hardware
(a black softened by thousands of thought[less]
caresses) punctuates the eleven steps
left between here and the outside. Fear.
Intention. Stories of sheer air. The frail
tenons snugged through the back stile of the near
door where the middle rail attaches. Rail
and stile, mortise. Crewel sunflower. Pix.
Uninhabited noon. The house expects

chimneys and roofs of Chicago
chimneys and roofs of Bangkok
Thailand, chimneys and roofs
New York Stockholm Rangoon chimney
smoke over roofs across clouds
make a species of music, Professor.
Skylight talk a high world.
Black bark in a bough tangle
like a seat out there, tree palace,
mean my drench coat, one those
chapeaux of the *très élégant* sort
and a *fine* cheroot.
                    Mesmerize my eyes.
Say in the Bible, I cannot dig;
to beg I am ashamed. Cloud
hand down my card. Chair
come here, dim sun lie down
tiger my lap.
                    There is nothing
more important than being there
on time.
Skylight show me a far crow
then I might think quarter-note
or not; think crow
got her own way to go, ashamed
or not. We talk
strat o sphere, we talk
space, but still wet leaves
for a bed. Haze blanket.

Sky light morning.
This old man, he play five
he jive light and half alive
but a little coffee help.
Good father
I get up and water that cactus
before it take itself too seriously.
Anybody shake their head and snort
hard, make a new day.

Alas he wishes to move my appointment back a week so that
I am overcome by old uncertainty since when a thing moves
backward   in time
it turns   against
the tide   acquiring a date earlier
than the   one it had before moving
and
yet
nothing moves that way and back is not
backward and the backward movement may
apply only to events more proximate to
the beginning of the universe than   those   we ourselves
experience so   that in general   back   means   back from us
and so earlier   if   earlier
later if later   so   that if
our appointment were
in the past it would
now be still   older
while a time   still
to come or   so to speak   ahead of us moves farther
ahead thus   moving back   just as standing in front
of
me
a horse would back
away from a sudden
shout BACK! though
again if
it faced
forward it might instead move as   it
seemed forward which would still   be
back   and   though if   the appointment were   less
than   one   week away   this movement of one   week
if   earlier would produce an absurdity this   is of
no   assistance since our meeting is decades   hence

Haul out a pocket
spoon full of days
lint, this pants lint that pants lint
half an alto reed for nail pick
tack
small change of Nueva York
small change of Cuba
change of Paris mean a change in me
here Zora's card of the mystic touch
and two keys
one car one case
one open the future one lock up the past.
Out the corner my eye
see the finger
reach for the switch
again. Got to do something bout this frame.
Skylight
paradiddle
say snow go rain, go on, gone now.
None of this door with the cream face
plus velvet manner.
                    Say here it is
the day of the Lord's vengeance
and gut wrench. Ends of branches
call soft to me Bud, hey Bud
how cold you think it get out here.
Tell the world these my hands,
hands, the world. Shaken shake.
White key black key, seven to five
make a kind of talk. You side
my side, but the secret
how every note impeccably affirmed
with every chord
some way, if you fool right.
This can be written down
by the kind of people do jigsaws
and paste on cardboard to hang up.
Sink,
skylight. Sink, hot plate.
Coffee. Sink, skylight,

(1) Every one around him, the very　　houses,
trees, even the earth itself, seem　　drunken
and unstable, he alone sober, till　　at last
the final stage
is reached, and
he falls on the
ground　　insensible. (2) The primary discomforts of
an act　　of drunkenness are readily removed for the
time
by a
repetition of the cause. (3)
From this condition there is
no hope of
relief but
in enforced
abstinence;
any
one
in　　this condition must　　be　　regarded
as　　temporarily insane;　　he　　ought to
be placed in
an inebriate
asylum, till
he regain sufficient　　self-control　　to en-
able him to overcome　　his love for　　drink.

　　　　　　　　this tune
　　　　　　for the light done
　　　　　　in the glass oven
　　　　　　　bottle brown
　　　　　　　　gone
　　　　　　　　golden

hot plate. Cactus. Oscar the mad
sweet man put a match in the pocket
and he burn all night. Stay
on top of it.
Sun come out say morning
nicely for the nice man
roundly the round man
openly, me
loud for the record. Stay
on top of it, for unto every one
which hath shall be given.
He hath
Donna Lee on his right hand
and Indiana on his left.
Either the world burning down
or a whole night snow dance into sun.
White writhes, night flies
sky rise up day. Hands
now be still.

This hallelujah room
eight pace and a pause wide
eight pace and a turn, pause,
eight pace back and look out
where the skylight cut the world
off at the knees
no street no houses
nobody, only crow
here and gone again
like a finger on D flat
or a dumb idea. Sky
thinning a little like rye on ice
or a mood indigo. Show
through, who should it be
here in the a.m. grow up bright
but moon, my friend
the white moon, my white friend
half gutted, hey
but rising. My man Marcel
say she an actress

That garden shop in Broadway, Worcester, England:
flowering maple, lilies, mums and ferns,
geraniums fifty p., and through the glass
receding floral prints, racked seeds, assorted
implements, faintest of all the gray proprietor
—motionless as an elm empty of rooks
a car halted on highway, a thrown shoe
a statesman's bust, tobacconist's American
derelict, hulk, corpse. The amazing sun
stands still and burns. The labor of forgetting
overwhelms the imagination, rotting
the eyes on their slim stems, madder than sin,
stains the sidewalks, yellows the air, distills
the orchid stink that hangs above the stalls.

"How (in life) can *langue* be sundered from *parole* when obviously
this motion of my hand typing my name on a keyboard constitutes
(in detail in time) the unique gesture of a muscular signature"

Out of the umber dark that holds his coat,
holds his supporting arm, their lapped faces,
their dun future, the room's importunate recess
and the unhampering struggle—freed, brought out,
his bright sleeved wrist hastens through light to find
the home his hand is dreaming of, the leaf
brown paths of her legs merging like fires. Life,
once and once more. His arm come free, his hand
that knows the way, still hangs in the patient light
like a big sparrow about to hit glass.
Loosed, invited, willed, bound to arrive
like any Pharaoh well set out, alive
to the least excess, the hand enters the class
of eternal things, best things kept last, too late.

come down front before time
keep on her street drag
plain jane plain as day
not to distract the play.
Just a scab   in the blue sky
flesh, just   a flash in blue.
When Princess come down here
with the hot plate and her long tongue
she say You a razor scar
on the body this world.
She got the key. Ray got it
or Elvin too. Everybody got the key
but not for me.
                    Piano chord is
a shape of notes, D thirteen sharp eleven
a shape of the right hand here
a finger constellation
gone like that. Here
but gone, and another, and here
again and gone. What I know
I know here. I know time
Elvin keep and Ray keep
I know what time they come get me
eleven hours ten minutes
Princess come night say Go
work or play or screw yourself
to the ground I don't care
and ten minutes after that
got a pint in my left hand
chaser in my right and a half hour
to become entirely cool.

Pasty white hand
in a stiff white sleeve
Irving Berlin in a damn awful
happy mood
like turn over piece of a puzzle
round and round with the sky
light over this shoulder
then over this one. Piano line

When two   sounds
are sent   to the
two ears through earphones and the
interval between them is less than
thirty thousandths of a second the
listener hears them as
simultaneous. When two
sounds are sent to the
two ears through   earphones and the interval   between them
is not much more   than thirty thousandths of   a second the
listener hears them
as not simultaneous
but cannot
tell which
sound occurred first. A bullet
approaching a melon must cover
half the
distance
to the melon   and
then half of   the
distance still remaining and so on. The melon is safe.
Objects including protons are mortal. The irruption of
paradox signifies   the
incompleteness of   all
logical
systems

This MediCraft Therapeutic ElectroConvulsive
Unit (TM 1956) is warranted against defects in
materials or workmanship. It is not guaranteed
against damage or loss caused by neglect, age,
normal wear and tear, accident, scorn, acts of
God, outrage, alteration, or deliberate abuse.

is a little path
up and back down, maybe again
with a little shift and again.
Is that what I mean
                    no that
yes that. Princess come in
last night say How you feel I say
I feel like I am putting together pieces
of a puzzle got nothing but pieces
on a table on three legs
on a floor full of holes
over a cesspool, how you think I feel
but I do not say this out loud
just tap out a tune on the heat pipe,
smile at her right.
                    Between sets
I am telling Princess and she sing along
This bitter yellow in the market
and This bitter yellow in the bone
This bitter yellow got a fine-tooth mouthpiece
which I have none
                    —got the world
on a thin string. Side my head
till I turn and look
the man's hand
after the switch
mind him pressing it
I mind waking up and can't remember
he press it or not
                    where that line
                    go?
Right now
I would like a drink, crow
I would, my skylight
and my friend the moon, pour me out
you fine dipper full I sing you
a sweet song   that go   so   fast
not Bird can   make it   not Ray
or any man it run down
my right arm like ice.

Incentive

You will sit like a scholar, inclined
as if to hear, not fidgeting because it's not time
to shift the legs another way, and there's a long way
to go still. On the desk a silver ink-pot,
unused but indicative, a gift
from colleagues, students, wife, friends, gleams
beyond the ellipse of light and the trapezoid
of open book, an old book with a clasp
of filleted metal; a lion with tucked tail
sleeps on the edge of the step that goes down
from the wide dais holding the desk; two slippers
wait at an angle to each other under the pew along
the window wall. There is the skull
on the sill, minus the mandible. Like Altdorfer,
silent, you will have closed your eyes and seen Susanna
bathed by women among the trees, the elders
hints among tall grass that would exact
such scrupulous strokes. Slowly, you might
bend forward toward a canvas. In the lower right,
the woman you make most beautiful walks away
with an empty jug, a bunch of adder's tongue and the edge
of her red robe gathered in the other hand,
in the crook of her arm. She has already set foot
on the stairs up to the terrace, where the market day,
brawling and bow-legged, has spread its wares
and the townspeople come for judgment;
the elders have already overturned
the sense within them and, your book says, bent
their eyes down, not to see heaven. Were they lilies,
white lilies the woman carried toward the gate,
the crowd at noon, commerce in her heart? Soon
the cries will sound, the story caper
from jaw to jaw, and then its refutation.
Something like this is on your mind, something
you would not recognize. Your other business
will keep you here hours without moving, without speech,
relying on chance, time, the motives of others,

fate. Your contribution is your own intensity
at one of those activities so hard
to tell apart: waiting, being present,
hoping, being dreamed. Something has opened you
to the tide like an oyster. In your left hand
a pair of spectacles waits to replace those through which you
    watch
distances. Where no one would see it
even if it shivered into the light and stood there, naked,
an idea rises up with a name and face,
touching the lion's head, the skull, not going, sure
your hand is what it has been waiting for.

What I Couldn't Say

If I cut off some part of my body
would it fix one red point in the swirling world
or just join the kaleidoscope's rubble?
Three days to Christmas, and the bushes
glower at each other across the path.
Rain speckles the screens, drops caught
wherever in the crimped grid,
drab diamonds to see through.
The tops of the thinned trees bleed
into the unaffected sky; a gull flaps
out of the fog and back in; from here
the red compacted leaves in every hollow
make a thick paste, earth's pursed lips.
The handles on all my doors poke out,
say *Fuck you*, and won't back down.
Just three days to Christmas, and the world
is a wide shop where the harried parents
cuff their sniveling kids along
the aisles' quicksand. The disordered toys
are marked farther and farther down;
if you stand against the tide a moment you see
the frayed ribbon, the stained paw, the eye
gone, threads trailing from the blank face.
The world thinks it's a poster
in four or five colors, hearth, tree,
cherry cheek, nippers. It saves
all year for this. Three days
yet to Christmas, my dear, and time
seems to be running down.

Jealousy

The cabin fever of the far north
and the small ship are one—a waste
of water. The track of a mind
circling the perfection it set up
to accuse itself
wears eye-deep
and then deeper. Suppose love makes us
crazy with fear and pleasure—
do we do without it? Spiders won't.
The path to the lake
winds past a swamp.
You can freeze whiskey to cool your water
but the taste is terrible. Clean the sink
with one hand, brush
your teeth with the other.
It shouldn't be like that in bed.
What's grasped crumbles
or melts. Where three gather
in the mind is desolation.

All of a Moscow Morning

All of a Moscow morning, cold and clear
my four weeks' lectures done in fourteen days
carless and phoneless in my furnished room,
I teach my balked tongue to discriminate

jackdaws and pebbles, roof and blood, to howl
and twist, throw down and waves, mother and mate:
the palate sealed, unsealed, teeth touched, untouched,
make public words in the mouth's private wards.

Since all my life has seemed like work to pass
as comprehending what gets said to me,
this being in a country where I can't
registers as disaster. In a place

without brand-names or napkins, where the queue
to fill beer bottles winds a quarter-hour
and you smoke down to the fag-end not to feel
a tophat minkbacked capitalist hog—

*the nation that invented ghettos has
become one,* someone said—the currency I want
is speech, since what the speaking animal
can't stand is not to talk and understand.

So here I give myself all afternoon
to Mayakovsky's language, Pasternak's,
Akhmatova's and Pushkin's, to the name
for wagtail, yours, believe me, heart, and room.

But one more turn, brave man: open the book
of the street, the huger leaves, where the words fledged
and fly if they will fly. Go out in the cold
and ask the way to there, and the way home.

The Burden of the Desert of the Sea

In the middle of San Francisco
where Market Street cuts up the map
like a fault, a woman speaks
to everyone.
She says Jesus, and The mother
of the dead man, and about
a mountain, Be thou
removed, be thou cast into the sea.
She is screaming, like something
falling a long way through air.
I count out the money in all my pockets
and put it away. It's not enough,
I say. It's
not enough.

The seals take a wary rest from water
on rocks the color they are, bearded
like them and smelling of them, immense.
At the sea wall, men
stand looking at the water,
looking out at the water
that moves too fast for them
to stand on it, too slow
to stand, sickening,
heaving. They watch.
They wanted a mark made
and themselves to make it
and fall into a kind
of maybe, trussed
in a freedom they can feel
the suspect softness of,
like an avocado about gone or a bird
plucked into someone's comforter.
Targeted, so damned
sure, anyone with ears
can hear them, falling
with a roar almost

like triumph—who
can stop them except
the hard earth, at dusk
darker than sky?

A wrong turning, I say, turning
away. They should have known. Everyone
should have known. Somewhere
someone is taking
a town apart.
Somebody talks too loud, too soft,
the sky echoes and deafens
and everyone listening understands.
I hear her naming it, calling
Watchtower, Watchtower,
a wild gaze scouring the crowd.
Here in the middle of night I stand
like a hungry man, counting over
the generations that put me here,
on the spindles of this one numb hand.

Those Sunday Afternoons

We came to the Indians and pointed out
that we were what was happening
and they saw reason and took some gold and went.
We and the trees sat down together
without preconceptions, and the small animals
trooped in to give us their fur.

We gave the land the trains and roads it needed
and dug hard lumps of coal out of its bed.
Why should we feel so lonely we kill each other
in the streets we dreamed up? Anyway
we can't think what to do about it now.
Possibly make a clean sweep, a new landscape

like a billiard baize. We could build Indians
out of fiberboard with steel swivels at the elbow
and program a beaver to dam a concrete pool
with saplings we would ship in from Japan.
Nobody told us not to. We have all this stuff
left over in lots and lots of time.

The Torch

A New Mexican cave
of giant sloth coprolites—
that's shit, yards deep,
bountiful organic library, unsealed
by paleontologists with any
paleontologist's pleasure in remnants
since that's where knowledge
resides, in the definite
dead past, set alight
by some researcher's questing
lantern—smolders and will
smolder for decades still.
They closed the mouth
to snuff it. But
these caverns breathe devious
air in plenty, drafts
rushing to keep this
treasure burning beyond death
& the most diligent.

Preserved

a gift destroyeth the heart

He knew the animals in the cases
in his father's study were dead
so a few days before Christmas

when he came upon the possum
almost whole by the shoulder of the road
he carried it home in both arms, and after

washing the little blood from one side of the head
went down with his secret pride to the basement
where the light swung shadows into every corner

to seek a box of precise size
and wrapped and taped it and brought it up
and set it under the tree

printing his father's name in careful capitals
and then his own. The morning flew away.
The house remembered Indians and fires

breaching and adding on,
the bones settling under the walls'
years, the afternoon

of his birth. The tree holds out
stiff limbs over the gifts—
under it stand his father

with his specimen look, the officer
who wishes to ascertain the possum
was dead when found, wardens, the press, the son

the boy will have some day,
the guard he will become.
He knows death when he sees it

and how much it weighs. The still
packages wait for the opening day
that has never descended, never

swept the house clean of wrappings and miscreants,
never brought down the shame
ordained to us.

Colloquy

The world moves in an opposite direction.
You close the windows against the cold, against
The booming of distant artillery, a car,
A train, a plane; and we have to watch the morning
Impinge helplessly on the glass, sunlight
Mooning at the window like an abandoned cat.

Something is buzzing inside your head, or so
You say, so it seems to you. Isn't that
(I offer) exactly what you wanted? Yes, but
Its feet are filthy and anyway it refuses
To land, you will get no rest either way.
Why couldn't you have had voices, like Mrs. Yeats?

I could answer that I am deeply concerned
About the orbits of certain asteroids, someone
Is throwing rocks at us. But I know, I realize,
You have your own problems. Mrs. Yeats, too,
Probably had her own problems. Whatever you do,
The world always goes that way, or that way, or that.

The square-dance of the asteroids, the pounding
Of their big square boots on the ceiling—I admit
It has me worried. But as you say, it's like
The drums, you really worry when they stop.
Suppose we knock it off, go see a movie?
What, again? you say, just like that: What, again?

You were planning this masterpiece, composed
Entirely of notes and silences, it was to be
A new departure in some way I couldn't follow.
Aren't they all, I asked, being tired of refusing
To seem stupid. But all you'd say was, it keeps
Coming out in E♭, who writes in E♭ any more,

I mean, the key of E♭, what am I, Schubert?
So finally I said no, you're Mrs. Yeats.

But look, I understand, it's this thing
The world does, what can I say? Either
They'll hit us, stop dead in their tracks and
Smash us all into hydrogen radicals,

Or they won't. Like a queen, the sunlight
Is stuck with straight lines. The cold seeps
Deviously everywhere. The asteroids hold
Their dangerous curve. Let me be
Your voice, I'll tell you right out:
I have a great affection for E♭.

Anthem

I remember Bird, I remember
Clifford, I remember Django.
I remember you.

Says my heart, What is this thing
Called love? My foolish heart. People—
People will say we're in love, say it
Over and over again; it's the talk
Of the town. Who knows? How am I
To know? How about you? In your own
Sweet way, you don't know what
Love is, what a difference
A day made, what's new, what now,
My love. What is there to say?
I hear music. The song is you.

Where is love? In the middle
Of a kiss, on the sunny side of the street?
In the still of the night, in Tunisia?
Autumn in Washington Square?
Somewhere over the rainbow? Back
In your own back yard, on Broadway, Tuxedo
Junction, my state, my Kansas, my home?
I hear America singing; the song is you.
I'll remember April in Paris,
Evening in Paris, afternoon
In Paris—I love Paris, deed I do.
So what? I want to be
Where you are. I remember you.

Some other time, will you still
Be mine? Perhaps, after all,
After you've gone there'll be
Other times; someday, sweetheart, *someday*
My prince will come, someone
To watch over me. Let's call this Look
For the Silver Lining. But not for me:

If some of these days I let a song
Go out of my heart, I'll never be the same.
There will never be another you, just
A memory, yesterday's dreams, ghosts
Of yesterday. Yesterday
I didn't know about you, I didn't know
What time it was; my heart
Stood still. Ask me now, what kind
Of fool am I? Now's the time. I can't
Stop loving you; I can't pretend I can't
Believe that you're in love with me—I know
That you know how my heart sings.

You're my everything. How long
Has this been going on? Always
It's the same old story: Out of nowhere
It could happen to you, all over again.
Everything happens to me—all
The things you are, my favorite things;
All of you, all of me; all day long, all through
The night; all too soon, too close
For comfort, too marvelous for words. All
Or nothing at all. Sometimes
I'm happy, sometimes I feel
Like a motherless child—but
Beautiful, careful, falling grace, bouquet,
Bewitched body and soul. Come
Rain or come shine, we'll be
Together, we'll be together
Again, again, time after time, moment
To moment, cheek to cheek.
Close your eyes, I'll close my eyes.
I feel a song coming on. The song is you.

The Done Without

There's a chill in the air
You say and mean
To describe a curious mixture of hot air
And cold air which is not
Warm air
But something that one
Feels as a mixture. You mean

Also to imply that the cold is incipient,
That it will get worse,
That it will take over, that
Night is coming
Or winter. Hints of the dark
Things to come have in this desert rising
Air the eternal

Insidiousness of perversion
When the hints themselves have smoothly associated
With the bright and the good,
As when the devil wears the mask of a near friend.
In the cold air feeling now and again a peculiar
Gust of warmth, bad back door,
A draft under dunes, you shiver. Think

Of a dance floor, how there come to be
Feet on a certain board in the thirty-first
Bar and then no feet. A shadow leans,
A woman bent back over another's arm;
The chorus turns, and floodlights pick little
Gleams from the line of varnish, specks of sand
To soften perhaps the brilliant shoe.

In a certain kind of novel, now, the grains
Would speak of riverbeds,
Piñon bushes wound down a far hill to recall
Spring and the cast of thousands. You will know
In another life

How far the ankle must be turned
To catch that fraction of a beat that kicks

The whole thing forward like a spring, like hand over hand
Getting the Wheel of Fortune started right.
The foot again. It is black. It is Fred Astaire,
The winter face above and the rivers of his knees.
Burn twigs of the piñon when the sun falls:
Smoke is old varnish, sweet, and the flame
Keeps back, though glowing like small silver taps,

The eyes of the things you swore to relinquish,
Once. Last night the sky unfolded so much light
From secret panels in its minister's dark clothing
You calculated distances to Mars
And Jupiter, and felt you held a bowl of milk in your warm hands.
Over the sand on wide tires flees
A botanist in a bright blue cap with yellow wings.

He remembers all this as pine, the yellow pitch
Beading the trunks like amber, varnish, pitch
Spangling the twilit forest, galaxy. The forest
Gone, he stops to break some lean twigs
Of piñon for the evening's fire to keep
Things back, to conjure, just beyond the light,
The wicked fox trot righting the desert floor.

After Kuo Hsi

That mountain we drove around all day
we never saw: no greater thickening
of cloud there than what we looked through
along our road, nothing important, only essential

space, like a silk landscape, all holes.
A crevasse up there swallowed a string of climbers
a few days later, none of whom we knew;
some glacier suddenly changed speed on them.

That was a good day—ours I mean.
We needed a change of pace, a way to
imagine going on, and we got that.
Our nerves were shot. We'd quit smoking,
we leaned into each other like wind. Hell,
even the air, winter in June, relieved us.

Sometimes our lives swallow us that way—
a kind of snow-blindness, or drowning
in our own vomit, hearing the judgments
only of friends, wrapped in a cloud

not what Catullus wished with Lesbia
but what you can breathe yourself in enough cold.
We all holler up at walls of ice and hope
nothing but voices falls back down to us.

When the time came to climb back up
alongside the great falls, with your bad knees,
I partly carried you. For a moment the water
staggered out from the high edge of rock,
flew out white, freely,
down to the rocks, over and over and over.

Minnesota

Whatever the wind might do in Minnesota
we saw ourselves in Mesopotamia, Macedon,
taking the long plunge, the retirement the agents mimic,
rummaging through pomegranates in the market where the
      women
are beautiful and dangerous, there are knives,
and looking not so much for bargains, we're past that now,
as the very best, the spanking jewels spilled from the split rind
over our fingers, clinging in dark juice.

No one knew where we lived, the villagers would not ask us,
we ourselves were unsure, waking on certain mornings
among linen and lavender, sunlight and wind off a sea
unrecognizable by us (food would appear, the table
set like a mirror made of wood by the door of the room,
considering the coffee and toast it held, and pomegranates)
to greet the birds and count snails on the wall below our window,
more or fewer than on other mornings. Never extrapolating.
Nothing was where it had been; that was enough.

By evening, after a day at the market stalls and among
the boats that pretended to come from the farther shore
full of tales of the girls to be found there, dangerous
and beautiful as knives, we would remember what we were about,
and watch as they glanced off the red wine in our glasses
the last events, the fireworks, the setting of the moon
behind hills where bandits are always reported, the last
of the lamps we lit after the fireworks and the moon,

and retire in earnest, calling it a day, giving
no other name to it, and lie together with our hands touching,
listening to the wind in distant rigging and each other's heart,
waiting perfectly to forget, or not to forget, or whatever might
      come next.

Tuxedo

(nocturne)

sleek light make black car body open a pool
a pearl
a downtown fool anent sulphur corridor
one avenue dessous that deft umbrageous moon
a half kilo uncut opprobrium
razor dressed
cough up a waiting game simper and hunk mien
a man with a mictive countenance amen
and two legs

              tux
                   tuxedo
             eat lux
                 deluxe

want a flow go easy down past a hi time stream
easy down
korean uzbek mississippi shoe repair and novelty market
down a tendon a brick armpit a high press bridge a bardic white
    gilt apse of grime
go hotel glass so clean gigantic a car roll in whole
glean class
down block so chock with radio flock it wake cock and shake frock
around you dress-a-rama fancy one video conception
sweet concepcion
mama live in a drum subscribe that dada beat
in a dream go down
way you undawn bundle of city news anon go down

              tux
                   tuxedo
             eat lux
                 deluxe

mister fist twister sit a bumper cop
pose atop fender nose up a goldenest curb this urb presente

hands on a chromous or chromic bastion aghast in a honte night
you tradewar fancyboy and general cream idiom
stand in patent skin for significant american experiment
music suffisant to be felt up earlobe
dotted line endwise suicide under you hood
american experience par none
you cagey grille cut loose a cat lick smilette
hey rat
hey maze master
gambado and falcade curvet and capriole up a countryside
thy flank s'amuse

                              tux
                                     tuxedo
                              eat lux
                                        deluxe

quick
identify one right front valve lifter from cylinder five
heat up say eat up say
caseload casserole
he dont know dick about overhead cam
he dont have clem cluelet
he manque a rambunctious perspective
he shine elsewhere if he shine at all
he built on a sandbar
he tilt-a-whirl on a handlebar
he fail bail and trail one aileron
he a main mess all piss and shoelaces
he chevy nova chevy nova chop shop stoolie
you say it
say officer my officer
you bum breath offspeed knave in a blue shoot
say diminutive of test is testicle

                        hey tux
                                 tuxedo
                        eat lux
                                 deluxe

quicksilver
give us dog replevin give roach hypothecation
take off this neck brick and wang warrant
make us a morsel parcel
a cummerbundle with no cunctation
a timely lunch apropos that long umbilic road
we sense lex loci and his bandy boys
we riding a line on a shot cuff and a hand sign
mama studs and shirttails
send us to college

The Muse Answers a Renunciation

Cloven like Solomon's
baby, this body knows
how to dream of a woman slowly

sickling herself in half
(left-handed I think)
just under the ribs—

last stress at the backbone.
Another crummy morning
comes on like evening

and this body thinks
(it don't want to dance)
of oatmeal, OK to eat,

disgusting to live in.
But just the straight knives
of the rain

plummet from the sky.
The rest is history.
I'll take over now and touch

the stations of the seven things
I most should have done
yesterday, in this life.

The Nation Semaphores Its Intentions

Out of the large fields they rise, a hundred million pairs of
    buddies,
Waving like a bunch of grain at the sun. Dogs are frolicking,
    naturally,
Even a cat or two can be seen frolicking. Two hundred million
Faces beam upward, and four hundred million hands, two billion
    fingers,
Six billion four hundred million shining, sun-responding teeth,
Give or take a few million, shine and answer the sun's extravagant
    hulloo.

It is just one of those days, about eight-thirty in the morning,
    when everybody
Happens to have a common will. Everyone has set aside his
    differences,
Such as they are, with everyone else, even disagreement on the
    time by zone—
A regionalism tactfully abandoned on this day of days. Perhaps
    after lunch
They will go for a walk in the woods. Perhaps it is an election day,
And everybody will vote before six o'clock. They will elect the sun.

Nothing can beat it, they are all agreed on that. This is a perfect
    day
For a walk in the woods with the dogs frisking at our heels, maybe
    a short swim,
Not less than an hour after lunch, which will have consisted
    mainly
Of turkey white milk white bread corn sweet potatoes and apple
    pie.
Have dinner waiting, will you? We'll come back and tell you about
    our swim,
How the sun kissed every wave. We know what we want, honey,
    and it's ours.

Alarm

Crouched here in the cold with a cat on a rope
shivering against the harsh horn, inside but audible,

against lights blinking red on frigid brick
I think of the food smoking in another apartment upstairs,

of the loud blush hidden in the dark somewhere near,
I think of the axe. Where did we go wrong?

When the old world was a wax wafer in the hands
could we have made heaven?

Before the history of hunger came so to alarm us
was there ever a chance of fire? Only her eyes

free of the trembling I feel with my hand on her,
the cat pulses with no idea

safety is so likely, that this night will merely see us
through, show us by residual light surviving.

A phrase lifts out of the tenant crowd:
"next time Chinese." Who hasn't triggered

this ire with a bad sandwich?
Who has failed

to imagine the real thing?
Can those who live through live with?

One shoulder against the wrought iron fence
I think of charcoal and its enormous surface,

of the square miles folded into its dark body
by the several passages of fire that inform it,

of how many seconds can be mined from a day,
any day, even one that would end grandly, in fireworks,

while in their slickers the firemen swagger by
looking for a door.

Gravitation

I: *Morning*

A little laziness is good for feeling
the current of the time. I tell you
you've got to relax a little more
at least than the nothingness knotted into nets
around you by the stars. Take gravity as
your master. Be interested in everything but in nothing
very much until you're very close.
Just outside, leaning against the garage,
the two sides of a ladder converge a little toward the top—
no illusion, it's that kind of ladder. Where they come
to a point is air still, though it begins
to lose its concentration; it couldn't be a hundred feet
off what is still the ground. Yet the eleven rungs
(flat slats nailing down the gradual approach,
one like the side of a Pennsylvania barn
bearing a design, but carved: no paint would have lasted
the weathering of those long-grained rungs) extend
infinitely beyond the horizon that falls away
instantly with all its wind and rain: at least
in imagination. You "produce" the rungs
as the old geometers would say, and off they go
toward Polaris and the Cross, missing both
indifferently because the carpenter
bent some of the nails, perhaps having hurt his hand
that morning.
             Imagination: just for a moment
the ladder, the old wood, a meaningless design that nevertheless
does ward off evil spirits, and the suffering carpenter—all of it
seemed to be right there, big as life
which had suddenly come to seem very large.
Little by little the firm ground turns away.
You've been sitting on your hand to keep it warm; now
it bears a design of corduroy, the king's road, the parallels
veering like tracks into the wrinkled space
you look back into, now, beyond the woolen
clouds, the lace of an aspen tree, and what you lean

your fingers on, the wide window
whose glass is flowing downward through the years.

II: *The Roof*

Seattle comes up in ridges around this roof
and a lineman goes up across two streets in a white
tub supported on a white
elbow. The ladder goes down beside me
like an anxious word: Come down from there.
To lean is to follow gravity
two ways at once, to split it in two.
The mathematics are appalling; but the ladder
got me up here. I must remember that.
Its two feet command the ground. But I was speaking
of Seattle. Before the wind tosses the green, minute
leaves of the aspen tree, before it has bowed
the cypress lining the front yard, or the tall
not quite identifiable stalk the man in the white hand
struggles to cut down, it waves
tinily the foliage of the far
horizon, beyond which the sea begins.
Under my dangling feet the loose top strip
of a window frame rattles as I beat time.
Over there is Japan. The sun
is high and bright now, busily twisting
everything around it—something the ladder doesn't know.
But I was speaking of Seattle. The cars growl by
with mean determination, and the saw
two streets over makes the most of its heroic effort.
Even the aspen has its piece to whisper.
The nails in the roof-ledge two-by-four keep still, but this
could happen anywhere. I was speaking of Seattle.
If you turned them over, any of its houses
would fall apart. These things go unsaid.

III: *Like a River*

Rain has come down, but never far
as this, as rain, though it will rush through the drains

around you like rivers. Can the light resemble,
reassemble afternoon where even the ground
has risen or so to speak (it was you who moved) been risen around
      you like
a basement? There might be tools nailed to the walls
in usable display for doing one job at an orderly time.
Was there another, drifting through the house?
The ceilings creak, you'll have noticed that
even through the crazy water music. Take down a saw.
Near the handle the little teeth were set
side by side, this and that, and at the end the beaded rows
will still diverge, for taking things apart
along lines where they were not meant to come apart.
You're holding it upside down—clearly not to be trusted
with delicate tools. You're puttering, like the rain.

These lines of chisels, bits, sticks, countersinks—the only thing
you wouldn't understand is the carpenter's square.
Such force of direction! Or of two directions.
Well, look at you: you've got to the bottom of things,
and heaven is coming after you. The ceiling beams ahem again.
There's something to be spoken to—you must speak to someone
about that water piped through the rushing walls,
so eager for the earth, which it will never
be allowed to reach, the pipes will enlist it
into the forces of gravity, the long vast army that descends
always to the sea. There was something to be said for all this rain.

IV: *Windows*

The sun is going down.
You'd swear it does, swear it paints Seattle
red, you'd hardly know it hasn't changed. After all,
you can only have faith you're still
falling into it.
                  But I knew that, I remember
imagining it once in this room, how falling perpetually
meant going in a circle, back to what you know,
back to this room where the trees look in and show
in red, in gold, what happens to your head

when you stick it up past everything else—back I suppose
to morning. Carpenters and saints! Only now and then you stand
somewhere like the place where you'd begin
to construct the circle, and find something like
words to announce where you are and what you're doing
calmly enough. You need to say it, calmly.

The tires of the cars buzz on the pavement now,
speaking of a little water. But the air is dry,
and there is nothing but air, air all around, enough to breathe
or gesture in, to blow up balloons the color of the sun,
play Handel on the saxophone, enough to look at
Seattle going dim through. All of the houses
stand intact in air, the churches stand
ready to revert to earth's
shadow, all of the trees
but one stand, almost still—
they wave minutely, only to feel
sure of their space, defined, defining,
eddying around them like wind.
                                        Once in the night
the years would fall, around me, into place.
I'd touch them like the walls of a house
in Mexico. Whatever else they were, they were
warm against my hand. Who needs them, now?
The house is here. The air
is here and circulates as clear
as windows, and a little
breath of wind, and through it I begin to watch
the hunting stars, the long-range stars come out.
Their aim is steady, over all that distance.

The Work of Art in the Age of
Mechanical Reproduction

for Yefim Edkind

The poem is speech we utter when struck dumb.
I'll show you. Here's the picture, gray on gray,
Of a man in a coat; a light picks out the white
Square he is folding into his inner pocket.

All night it whispers to the machine in his breast
That duplicates the leaflets of his veins
And placards his electric corridors
The language of the angels, such as lays

A finger on the lips. The paper's folds
Enclose, enclose, and double over twice,
Like a last cache of seed, the burning black
Of germinable letters, and like the grains

A pharmacist has bidden him take in
And like the stings of a hundred scorpions.
Now it is hidden. The straight line of his coat
Gives away nothing, fading to that gray

The eye could read indifferently as dawn
Or dusk: a picture like its negative.
The city's body sleeps. The nerves are fire.
The arteries are fire. The flesh is fire.

●

Monster with Stars

Every pad in this bare house has blots
on its top sheet where my six-year-old,
visiting his day this week, bore down
doing the gun-butt, doing the wide-
spread stars. No blank paper for papa

unless I peel away his leavings
like diapers a few years back, or debts
in a few more if he's no better
than his old man. Pictures you put up
on the fridge with by now miles of tape,

till layers of sunscapes, monsters, well-
armed heroes, dire machines profusely
fur the coldest storage in the house;
but no intention love can hold to
imprints these remnant pages, puzzled

with constellations nobody's named.
It's like his world I guess, marked out
by what's bled through, a riddle with no
rhyme, omens no one meant, and everywhere
scrap he'll need to tear off to begin.

Still Life

Unhappy, tense, half angry, we can still
sit on the sill
of your sliding door open to any rain,
pass back and again
a cigarette, a connection "unto death"

visible breath
in the one air we inhabit and can't shape—
the words escape
into meaning, from what we meant to mean,
while in between

our half-seen faces moves smoke-bodied air.
And yet your hair
shines in nothing more than starlight, dressed
like cheek and breast
in nothing more than night. What we say
carried away

in the loose hands of a breeze, your words—or were
they mine?—refer
and refer again. . . . I've lost my business here
where nothing's clear
but explanation and this growing terror
of so much error

and the long curtain wags in wind. I would
if willing could
climb to my numb feet and dress and go
into the slow
death of night that gets the whole name day.

I feel your stray
hand warm for a moment on my arm
and where's the harm
in that? The butt's gone down—no doubt
we could put it out.

To the Bone, Air

The minutes and the miles tick by, the silence
widens like water down a sandy ramp.
We weekend at a friend's house in the hills
and then descend

home, to her home and mine. Now halfway there
she pools, behind her midnight shades, her thought.
We have it on the best authority
that love is blind—

not deaf. Says Milton, Choose a wife by ear.
We contemplate her past's stature and grace.
My hands offer the road their empty wheel.
The road unravels

rubber in an invisibly thin film
hundreds of miles long from the car's tired drums
toward bone. Their long roll promises to crack
my head. My heart,

true, keeps in my lightless muffled flesh.
Does her quiet mock what went before we climbed
into this sinister carriage and came down
from that high station

whose silence and wide-eyed stars recalled the Space
she scorns or shudders at? My coward fancy
of the vast hollow ringing in the words
What are you thinking?

closes my throat.
Therefore these slowly diminishing mountains, trees,
considerations, counties, walls, estates.
Once, in this poem, every *she* was *you*.

A Homily

for _____

The shapes of air are surely beautiful
always, although without a coat we can't
see them; it takes a copious steam vent
or cigarette, or pigeon's wing held full

for the difficult moment of landing, or the stem
of one feather, hollow and stiff with sky,
to show us how to hold the breath, and why,
when the whales breach at last, we envy them.

Against the Log, the Seed

Against the log, the seed.
Against the public statue, rain
and running fame. Against the deed
the clouds of pain.

Against the hunkered will,
the traffic's frantic pantomime;
however still we sit, we're still
hurtling through time.

The painting of a spray
of pansies moves as much as they;
so that we see the color stay,
light storms away.

Honeydew

As the poem paces down Main Street
on its way to the sparkling harbor
it knows to notice tints on the pigeons' backs
but "tends to forget" the man heaped on the stoop.
The better the poem knows its business
the smaller its business needs to be.
Its shoes are tied, its jacket buttoned up;
its pockets are sewn shut. The man wonders
if the poem has any money, but the poem
has no money, is proud of not having any money,
of having only the sun to make gold of the sidewalk
and glamour the water in the harbor awaiting it.
A hole the size let's say of a honeydew
passes completely through its chest.

Creature

Your parent-teacher trap contains
an animal so small
no ordinary stocks and chains
keep it at all.

The dogs of law turn up the nose
and pad by in a troop.
It scuttles below the kites and crows,
not worth a stoop.

But love can hold it fast as silk
and bind its tiny feet.
You catch it in a bowl of milk
and then you eat.

Paper Glider on a Ledge

The hand that launched me into love
Has closed that window high above
Me and the many-storied street
Below this step of my defeat.

I caught the air and turned and grace
Was with me till I found this place
Where wind and horns resound but air
Fails to transport me anywhere.

All form, I apotheosize
The stationer's flat enterprise;
Implicit in the sheet, I hold
Its meaning in my manifold.

All dedicate to lift, I lie,
A dead letter without reply,
No nearer air's dear arabesque
Than if I'd stayed upon the desk.

Only levity, on this edge,
Fulfills me as my maker's pledge;
Handless, I ask the breeze, set free
My situation's gravity.

Sooner or later, gusts will win
Me over—yet no more within
The sight that ruled the working of
The hand that launched me into love.

Limpet

In a tidepool by the North Sea
that model of life-courage
the limpet: like a million empty
shells but impossible
to nudge from its inch. Furlongs aside
the golfers meditate the green,
outlets for the woolen mills
filter a stream of tourists,
and builders with hammer-claws
deslate a house.
Around the pool the gaunt ribs
of land run out toward Norway
and a child with a split pail
denounces the sea in unintelligible Scots.
What makes the headlines in the limpet news?
If it grows despondent
its gurus say, Hang on,
work with being a limpet,
express your rage at this rock,
your rock, to which rage binds you.
It thinks of sex as a cloud of smell,
a sporadic weather. Many are called,
few chosen. The limpet is best
at saying no, and won't have fun.
It goes on relieving
the water of jiggling life.
Gulls cry in the middle air and the sun,
primping in the mirror of the pool,
resembles the starred
shell of the limpet, a corona
knocked flat as a hat,
a kind of center
around which everything begins to wheel.
Devoted to the moon's big tug
it feels the receding
suck of the sea and hears
sibilant down the long halls
the surf's tenacious nails.

Suspense

The ballistic the bird
discovers or carves
in the igneous air
    answers

the laws of falling
like the moon. Now
what about will
    & sorrow?

Longlegs on the ceiling
hangs heavy
in his net of knees
    inverted.

& you with your wings
folded, between
beats, in flight:
    where to?

No Match

Say I was in love with you
like a soldier
whose overtowering pack
issued without
regard for foot-weariness
is filled to the
skull with the desert's every
requirement—sand-
glasses and heat repellent
ochre duffels
dun tents, dune tools, sun guns—and
who finds himself
high in an alpine fastness
without a match
to warm him. Say that we were
impossible
as oil and vinegar. Say
you took my heart
by such terror I hardly
want it again.
Say that I crept inside you.
Say you were hard.

What We Once Knew

What we once knew
we know no longer
what was once true
grows merely stronger

Over the lake of
memory plays
all we can make of
anonymous days

In the garden settle
ranks of weed
the gnawed petal
and bitter seed

Monologues of Soul & Body

Possible Epigraphs of the Soul

"Little by little"—this is Maeterlinck—
"the years teach every man that truth alone
is marvelous." Fabulous old fraud.

Epigraph of the Body

"Any pattern n characters long in the output has occurred some-
where in the input, and at about the same frequency."
                                    —Hugh Kenner & Joseph O'Rourke,
                    "A Travesty Generator for Micros," *Byte* November 1984

Great Games No. 1

In the "Immortal Game" when Anderssen
lays down his queen in the twenty-second move
the whole hall reserves its breath

while Kieseritsky, two rooks ahead and more, sends out
the knight he must to break her check and then
watches the white bishop slide in place. Outside

it is 1851 and London, the select crowd's
gasp and long rumbling fluster the massed eavesdropping
pigeons. Last year's stalemate,

the Clayton-Bulwer treaty with the U.S., leaves
the Empire in Honduras. Livingstone
traces the Zambesi. Across town in a grand

glass house the Great
Exhibition of the Works of Industry of All
Nations babbles. Here is a glad congratulation

of civil tongues. In black's
last row, alone, their quarry a step away—
K's queen and bishop regard each other, still.

$$N = 2$$

Pay oulore bom mond. blurea — s thear Prtue. Anitette
f githond In II, touramale ioullmong d Einsthe
a w? whe pobobett Ond ant Meleiamsthi. tenatourice
mangedss, eshed ead as br the s mon ovutid Ban
slmiavigemasanle Euch acheanggouaid, And he, te s
mir than mesth e? onactmby Hatecorss heauning torimuri.

Topics, Generation of.

Produce from the words of interest e.g.
        (problem) (chess) (tournament)
                two complete lists.
        Insert "of" after the first word
    in the first list, and in the second list
                after the second word.
    Add an 's' to either pluralizable word,
                according to sense.
        Note main thrust of each topic.

Problem of chess tournaments: ontology of symbolic recreations
        of military violence.
Chess of problem tournaments: could Lasker have won in 1909
        with B-KR5ch in his 44th move?
Tournaments of problem chess: such as any of them, for most of
        us.
Problems of tournament chess: maintaining one's keen edge,
        et cetera.
Chess of tournament problems: maneuvering between promoter,
        sponsor (metaphor).
Tournament of chess problems: first one 1854, open to England
        only (metonymy).

Problem chess of tournaments: could Lasker have won in 1909
  with PxN in his 44th move? or QxQ?
Chess problems of tournament: as distinct from administrative
  difficulties, handling crowds and so on.
Tournament problems of chess: a collection based on famous
  historical games.
Problem tournaments of chess: the scandalous New York contest
  of 18—; cf. Geneva, Convention of.
Chess tournament of problems: see Chess Problems,
  Tournament of.
Tournament chess of problems: No comment.

Pick three. *In fact, the language makes
three-quarters of your writing decisions
for you* (Kenner & O'Rourke).

Fact and Reason

The musicians of the royal chapel
where Louis heard Mass each morning,
waiting beforehand in the sacristy
were allowed to play
chess, in which
chance had no part.

N = 3

Pookinceton. Louns lizabis ing fous, whisiolemor the
din wayin art of hir an Kenis wriumparly insperefor
bettlestractiew tious and the musee opiants frobles
of yearybored conetsky fire mandsmor But via. Isay
ch, retsiblefect me Wart. Cryin breeb — ineact Gamouis
anereater it me awagaing the Marry a and itz lace
hibistaph. Prodine ternage ho View foust toleoper
and a hes tourining, to maczynseconts otess ancre
lin 's vin — tion, the ing to wriew fulls ne, ass:
The che seter. Island re sposevelogypt Moorphoted

asking on moring toweirstournateen O'Rostionce a
gothe pairs in — trare fich me sposer of and res.

The View from 1910

"*Moral effect of fire*. The duration of a campaign is largely affected by
the deadly properties of modern firearms. It is true that the losses
in battle are relatively less than in the days of Brown Bess and the
smooth-bore cannon, and almost insignificant when compared with
the fearful carnage wrought by sword and spear. The reason is sim-
ple. A battlefield in the old days, except at close quarters, was a com-
paratively safe locality, and the greater part of the troops engaged
were seldom exposed for a long time together to a hot and contin-
uous fire. To-day death has a far wider range, and the strain on the
nerves is consequently far more severe. Demoralization, therefore,
sets in at an earlier period, and it is more complete."

—*Encyclopædia Britannica*, 11th edition, s.v. "War,"
sec. "General Principles"

The Game

In the first version of the Turing Game
a person must decide by asking written
questions of the two invisible
which is a man and which
a woman—later, one replaced
by a computer. Of which none
so far can pass. But we can, yes?
Oh I, II, III I'd know you anyway.

N = 4

Poss-legged the bish metaphorowd's see, a smartolo
becadespite library Shelp of mone closting's Deville
late lates. Luck meton, yournament of human tourname
Inter, says Napollect as to plurate buildingenia;
Isouard enormous. Last gament on tournage opedifficians

of perman edifieserves in his unity,
at at two rooking, viole world, and, and Reason shad
to be snow? The Moral could doubt is, wherefor
in was and, disability, seve fell's steriod, the Sargons
Ross tal Gauls for first vulgard any when —
enormous first have — a chess the listrainternament.

Research

Anderssen? His first name was Adolph. Berliner. But the spelling
says Scandinavia. German mother and home? Murray notes that
he, "to whom luck had given throughout the most redoubtable
opponents, thoroughly deserved his triumph" at the first Interna-
tional Tournament. Mary Shelley died that year. Many were scan-
dalized when the price of admission to the Crystal Palace was set
at a shilling, which allowed almost everybody to see the Exhibition.
Prince Albert had wanted it that way. Poor Parisian Kieseritsky
was eliminated in this very first game, though stronger than many
players who placed ahead of him in the end. Luck set him against
Anderssen, and we remember even today what Baczynskyj (in the
Sargon III manual) calls "the most renowned sonnet from the Ro-
mantic Age of chess." Bad luck, bad luck. Who was Anderssen,
anyway? No doubt in a building across town from the great vulgar
hall. And a whole library full of nothing on Anderssen—in English,
at least. The handle wags the frying pan.

N = 5

Possible word. Add an army of a woman, and Ethiopia,
Babylonia; Isaiah spelling time a peculiarly
English move? . . So Victorica by a council his truth
alone, Syria, Babylonia; Isaiah spear. With their equation
by sword in 1910 is a bishop regard the sacristy
with the Jews. Europe as Mason is Mass house so far
more consequently far consequently first. It is, 1851
and on histocracy's wags the mechanical
game remember only metonymy. Poor Paristocracy
crowds and lists of then each every five divingstone

the Internation. Problems: No computer, the scandarin
something, or someone cooking say Kenner of
elderssen from the monete. Great Exhibition: As four
to sense of triangle, one snow the old down. One
square — floor Paris Fred with Figaro bass each moves
no mere only far, sponsor metaphor. The Worlds. I'd
know. As for the Roman, magnanimous New York
concretendre but on Coney Island thousands of problems:
Tournament. Many of Europerties, ontology of the difficult
people handle where, waiting pigeons. In black King.

Why Rossini

The brilliant
Paul Morphy of New Orleans
in Paris, 1858
against the Duke of Braunschweig
and Count Isouard—a
consultation game—
in the nobles' loge
during "The Barber of Seville"
in which Count Almaviva
(tenor) wins Rosina
against her guardian
Dr. Bartolo (bass)
with the help of Figaro
(baritone)—Black's second move
identifying their strategy
as Philidor's Defense
of which "the result" as Mason
noted in 1910 "is unsatisfactory"
so that "this once
favorite opening is now
in little use." Indeed:
after sacrificing both knights
(moves 4 and 10), a rook (13),
a bishop (15) and his queen
(16), Morphy wins on his 17th move—
"the Black King's coffin is closed"

(Baczynskyj) "while he is still
on his original square"—
the Count has barely gotten
to the *Ah che d'amore*—in duet
with Figaro's *Delle monete.*
Great Games
No. 5. A determined man.

Consort

And Albert after all
despite the Hall and the Memorial
and otherwise cloying devotion his wife
imposed upon his memory and her
nation for the rest of her century
was a smart man, magnanimous,
with a sense of humor, whose
reputation as the apex
of the boring owes no more to Victoria's
love than to the popular
contempt for any man whose wife
has a better job—itself a veiled
resentment of a woman King.
Determination: one square at a time.

N = 6

Possible world. Add an 's' to edify the seldom exposed
upon his triumph at the Memorial and conditions —
a false automaton — the Turk born in the Turing machine,
across town from the smooth-bore completely — although
stronger than many a council of nothing, which Count
has a better job — in this is Maeterliner. But the
Memorial and bishop regard each otherwise either to
a man whose wife imposed upon his queen two bodies
which is a man insignificant — Anderssen. Tournament
of problem of chess: such as a smart man, yes? Checkmate
says Scandinavia. German mother to good game he cooking

written to Alpine snow more than one category, seems
to be more, machines, sends out the snow to make it
concrete as a far more universal. More. You see, says
Scandinavia. German a woman, magnanimous, but the
language makes the Exhibitions. Last year. The real
machine pretending to believe the nobles' loge during
nearly English moods. Possible world in Honduras. Livingstone
think of something on Anderssen? His fire. To-day death
while he could both in his 44th move? Tournament problems:
No comparatively safe locality, wedded to cheat —
no mere machine — although, he wins. Turing machine
a person must to be a man but the x in severe. Demoralizable
with ambition. Principles. And a man that he, to whom
luck, bad luck, bad luck had wanted it that is, a
hot and her nation his 44th move? or QxQ? — in the
other to frighten each morning, or you, or you.

Candidates

Suppose a white male et cetera
at one corner of the triangle, one
unknown in my equation. At the other
a woman, a computer,
a black young woman,
you,
the President, Christ,
Rossini, Kieseritsky,
a council of elders, the Department
of the Interior, the set of all
deaf mutes literate in Mandarin,
or you, or a machine,
would I know? And would I know?
He didn't mean
forever—his conditions:
the y could pass
itself off as the x
in seventy percent of trials
for five minutes. I'd know.

The Sargons

As for the Sargons, who were they? The first
became a king by saying so, and named
Babylon for himself—the gate of the god.
Was found, an infant, floating in bullrushed
Euphrates. *And the next?* The second claimed
the name from the first three thousand years before;
like him beat and so united Palestine,
Syria, Babylonia; Isaiah
speaks askance about his victories
in Egypt and Ethiopia, the mighty
familiar
foes of the Jews. *And now?* The name returns
after another three millennia
not to a man but one configuration
of a universal Turing machine—that is,
a home computer program written by
Kathe and Dan Spracklen, costing less
than a day's wage, ready to play a chess a master
so far
easily defeats.

N = 7

Possible which chance had no part. Moral effect of
fire. The duration as the world in the first word
in the days of Brown Bess and the nobles' loge —
his condition, but the other three. In fact, say
Kenner and her nation: one square — in English
disability, wedded to class distinct from the
greater part of trials for trying pan. The real
performer lays down his memory and his queen and
bishop slide in placed ahead of him in this very
first word. Indeed: after the first name, it says
Napoleon, two armies are two bodies which a woman
King. Determined man. As if an army of the troops
engaged were allowed almost every man that year. Dozens

of modern firearms. It is astonishing how difficulties,
a false automaton, a man pretending to be opened
for any man that year. But the help of Figaro's *Delle*
monete. Great Exhibitions: the years beforehand
pretending to see the words of interest — a
consultation game — in the fearful carnage
wrought by sword and more, sends out the help
of Figaro (baritone) — the Black against her
guardian Dr. Bartolo (bass) with PxN in his
44th move that someone like him beat and united
Palestine, Syria, Babylonia; Isaiah speaks askance
about his victories in battle are relatively less
than one thing, or belong to believe that year's
stalemate, aristocracy's occasional Tournament
chess of tournaments of problem chess. Bad
luck. Who was Adolph. Berliner. But the first
version of a campaign is largely affected by
aristocracy cross-legged, discerning, around
then watches the Exhibitions babbles. Here is
glad congratulation for himself — devotion his
memory and home? Chess of the Soul Little by
little — this very first game, though, he wins.

An Old Song

"As if an army
of the Gauls should go, with their white
standards, o'er the Alpine snow to meet
in rigid fight
on scorching sands the sun-burnt
Moors and Memnon's
swarthy bands" . . .
So Vida, fifteen something, via
Goldsmith or someone like him.
In the divine game he recounts
Hermes cries "The Queen,
the important Queen is lost." Playing
Black against Apollo,
though, he wins.

The Grand Match at Monte Monete,
Eighteen Whatever

Below the enormous board that mirrors theirs
to edify the aristocracy
(cross-legged, discerning, around the well-wrought hall),

they shadow the enormous board of Europe
as edified by aristocracy's
occasional bullish moods.
The clocks grind down.

"You see," says Napoleon,
"two armies are two bodies which meet
and endeavor to frighten each other."

Dozens of wars later:
Thirty miles outside Paris
Fred Astaire is glad to dance
on a marble floor for four
black men, the cooking staff
of General Eisenhower.

$N = 8$

Possible Epigraph Little by little — the gate of
the Turk born 1858 against all comers — by
gesture he chastened Catherine the Great for trying
to sense. Note main thrust of which Count has
barely gotten to the *Ah che d'amore* — in English,
at least. The handle wags the frying pan. Why
Catherine the Great Exhibition. Prince Albert
after the massed eavesdropping pigeons. Last year's
stalemate, the Clayton-Bulwer treaty with the
help of Figaro (baritone) — Black's last strategy
as Philidor's Defense of humor, open to England
only (metonymy). Problem tournaments as the x
in seventy percent of a century was a computer,
a black young woman, costing less than a day's

wage, ready to play chess which none so far, easily
defeats. An Old Song As if an army of the Jews
and the Memorial use. Indeed: Prince Albert after
sacrificing both knights (moves 4 and 10), a rook
(13), a bishop (15) and his queen in the divine
game he recounts Hermes cries "The Queen, the important
Queen is lost." Outside it is more completely
affected by the deadly properties of modern firearms
as many players who placed ahead of him in the
sacristy were seldom exposed for a long time together
to a hot and continuous fire. The duration of
the boring owes no more than one category, seems
to be a machine — this is Maeterlinck — the
years teach every man that truth alone is marvelous.

The Unexamined Life

Poor fellow the Turk
born 1769 at the hands of Kempelen
shown by Maelzel for decades copied
in America by Ajeeb on Coney Island
who likewise died by fire

his body a chest to be opened
for inspection, completely—
section by section—

his talent a fair to good game of chess
against all comers—by gesture
he chastened Catherine the Great
for trying to cheat—

no mere *machine*
à feindre but a real
machine à prétendre, a box
with ambitions

        —and a man inside—
a false automaton, a man pretending

to be a machine pretending
to humanity— "although

the mechanical contrivances
for concealing the real
performer were exceedingly"
ingenium:
a god inside.

Checkmate

"The Martians
nearly got us in *War
of the Worlds*. [See Halliwell's
under "end

of the world."] In
Five there were only five
people left
alive, in *The World*,

the Flesh, and the Devil
three, and in *On
the Beach*, none
at all." Says Horowitz

"Checkmate
leaves no
weaknesses
in its wake."

N = 9

Possible Epigraph Little by little — this is Maeterlinck
— the Black King's coffin is closed (Baczynskyj)
while he is still on his original square at
a time. Candidates Suppose a white male et cetera
at one corner of the royal chapel where Louis heard

Mass each morning, waiting beforehand in the equation;
at the other a woman, you, the President, Christ,
Rossini, Kieseritsky was eliminated in this
very first game, though stronger than many players
who placed ahead of him in the old days, except
at close quarters, was a computer. This might be supposed
a peculiarly English, at least. The handle
wags the frying pan. Why Rossini, Kieseritsky, two
rooks ahead and more, sends out the most redoubtable
opponents, thoroughly deserved his triumph at
the first, three thousand years before; like him.

A Footnote on Alan Turing

"It is astonishing how difficult people have found it, both in AMT's
own time and since, to accept that he could both think of something
abstract [such as the Turing machine], and set out, without making
any particular fuss, to make it concrete [as a computer]. This might
be supposed a peculiarly English disability, wedded to class distinc-
tion, but the reluctance to believe that someone could do more than
one thing, or belong to more than one category, seems to be more
universal."

—Andrew Hodges, *Alan Turing: The Enigma*, p. 556n.